Adrian von Buttlar

NEUES
MUSEUM
BERLIN

Architectural Guide

Adrian von Buttlar

NEUES MUSEUM BERLIN

Architectural Guide

S M
B Staatliche Museen
zu Berlin

DEUTSCHER KUNSTVERLAG

1 The Neues Museum, 2009, west façade

INTRODUCTION

In October 2009, just over 150 years after its construction, the Neues Museum opened for a second time (fig. 1). Following the reconstruction of the Alte Nationalgalerie (2001) and the Bode Museum (2006), this marked a further step in the implementation of the master plan for conserving, restoring and modernising the Museum Island in Berlin. This unique ensemble of outstanding buildings and art collections in the historic centre of the former Prussian capital not only constitutes a major monument to the early evolution of public museums in Europe, but also reflects some hundred eventful years in the history of collecting and museums. For this reason UNESCO declared the Museum Island a World Heritage site in 1999. The worst of the war damage sustained by the other four museums on the Island was repaired in the two decades after 1945, but the Neues Museum, which had suffered particularly severely, survived in the post-war period as a crudely patched-up ruin with provisional functions. Only after German reunification in 1990 did it become possible to take serious steps towards conceiving, planning and carrying out its reconstruction. The project developed into a unique conservational, architectural and museological challenge.

From 2003 to 2009 the British architect David Chipperfield and his restoration consultant Julian Harrap created a masterpiece that, though not without controversy, has been acclaimed by specialists and the general public alike. On the one hand, it pioneers complex ways of preserving and repairing a building's historical remains with the aid of the latest conservation and restoration technology. On the other, its 'augmented rebuilding' employs a characteristically modern architectural vocabulary in adapting new sections to their historical surroundings. The new areas, replacing parts completely or partly destroyed by bombing or subsequent weathering, include the north-west wing and the south-east projection, along with façades, parts of the two courts, several rooms and sections of the interior decoration (fig. 62). In itself, this synthesis of opposites, this blending of past and present to form a vibrant new entity, is not a new way of engaging architecturally with historic buildings, but at the Neues Museum it has acquired an exceptionally spectacular and innovative quality. Some well-meaning architecture enthusiasts petitioned for a referendum to push through a meticulous reconstruction of the old Neues Museum. To understand why that was not feasible it is necessary to explain the nature and significance of the original building, erected from 1843 to 1859 to designs by Prussian court architect Friedrich August Stüler (1800–65), to examine the damage it suffered in the war and to elucidate current museum requirements and the ideas about conservation that informed the reconstruction.

HISTORY
AND SIGNIFICANCE

THE MUSEUM ISLAND

The idea of public art museums originated in the eighteenth century, during the Enlightenment, when royal
collections came to be seen no longer principally as man-
ifestations of power and superior taste, but as motors of
bourgeois education, aesthetic sensibility and national
identity. In July 1793 the revolutionary National Con-
stituent Assembly in France issued an edict proclaiming
the populace's right of access to national art treasures and
announcing the foundation of a central art museum (the
Louvre). Yet when the archaeologist Aloys Hirt presented a
plan for establishing a public museum in Berlin five years
later he was not so much responding to the French move
as continuing the tradition of progressive education policies pursued by Prussia's rulers. The scheme was not put
into practice immediately. Not until the disastrous defeat of
Prussia by Napoleon's troops in 1806–07 and the subsequent removal to Paris of the most famous works of art

(including Johann Gottfried Schadow's brand-new Quadriga of Victory atop the Brandenburg Gate) did the project mature. It eventually reached completion a few years after the end of the Napoleonic Wars, under King Friedrich Wilhelm III.

Karl Friedrich Schinkel's Lustgarten museum (1823–30) forms a cornerstone in the history of modern museums. Behind a neo-Greek hall featuring colossal columns and murals depicting the development of culture, it housed a collection of Antique sculpture on the lower floor and a picture gallery on the upper. Schinkel's building embodied a reinterpretation in architectural terms of the centre of power in Berlin. For the first time art played a highly visible role in the urban fabric, in accordance with Idealist aesthetics and, in particular, the educational and cultural policies of Wilhelm and Alexander von Humboldt. The museum asserted its presence directly opposite the royal palace and granted art a status as a pillar of the state equal to that of religion and military patriotism, represented by three other structures on the edge of the Lustgarten: Schinkel's remodelling of the cathedral, begun in 1816 and later replaced by Julius Raschdorff's neo-Baroque domed building of 1893 to 1905; Schinkel's Neue Wache on Unter den Linden, erected after the Napoleonic Wars; and the palace bridge, erected from 1819 to 1824/57 and featuring allegorical groups of dying warriors (fig. 2).

In 1841 the new king, Friedrich Wilhelm IV (reigned 1840–58), an enthusiastic patron of the arts, adopted a proposal made by his recently appointed director general of museums, Ignaz von Olfers (1793–1871), to turn the island between the river Spree and the Kupfergraben canal in the former Lustgarten into a '*Freistätte* for Art and Science'. The word *Freistätte* (free area), borrowed from legal terminology relating to the right of asylum, effectively created a dis-

2 Karl Friedrich Schinkel, View of the Lustgarten in Berlin with the Altes Museum, the cathedral, the palace and the palace bridge, 1823, drawing, Staatliche Museen zu Berlin, Kupferstichkabinett

trict outside local jurisdiction. Devoted to lofty didactic purposes, the area was to include a building with assembly and lecture halls for the Friedrich-Wilhelms-Universität, founded in 1809 and housed in the former residence of Prince Heinrich on Unter den Linden (and renamed Humboldt-Universität after the foundation of the German Democratic Republic in 1949), and a second museum, to be called 'Neues' (new) to distinguish it from Schinkel's 'Altes' (old). The overall arrangement, developed by Stüler from the king's ideas, has often been held to epitomise the notion of Berlin as an 'Athens on the Spree' and therefore to form a counterpart to the Acropolis (figs. 3, 4). In fact, with its temple-style buildings and its courts surrounded by colonnades, it bears a closer resemblance to the imperial forums of ancient Rome. This pedigree also explains why the plans for a central, large podium temple with Corinthi-

3 Friedrich Wilhelm IV, Sketch for the '*Freistätte* for Art and Science', 1841,
Staatliche Museen zu Berlin, Kupferstichkabinett

4 View across the Friedrichsbrücke to the Alte Nationalgalerie and the
Neues Museum, 1881

an columns was clung to long after the projected university structure had given way to plans for a third museum, the Nationalgalerie built by Johann Heinrich Strack from 1866 to 1876. Moreover, the imperial forums in Rome doubtless prompted the erection of an equestrian statue of the king in front of the museum–temple, linking the notion of a forum devoted to education and edification with traditional dynastic claims to sovereignty. This juxtaposition of a museum building with the statue of a ruler persisted when Ernst Eberhard von Ihne constructed his Kaiser Friedrich Museum (now called Bode Museum, after its renowned first director, Wilhelm von Bode) at the tip of the Museum Island from 1898 to 1904 (the statue of the emperor was destroyed in 1950). However, the latest of the museums, Alfred Messel and Ludwig Hoffmann's neoclassical Pergamon Museum, begun in 1909, was not completed until 1930, during the Weimar Republic, and reflects the new era following the overthrow of the monarchy.

THE OLD NEUES MUSEUM

It already became clear during the planning of the Altes Museum that Schinkel's building could not accommodate all the collections, not least as its primary focus was to be classically based original works of art. Holdings of Egyptian art, for example, accessible since 1835 in the small palace of Monbijou, had expanded enormously in the 1840s as a result of excavations undertaken under the aegis of Friedrich Wilhelm IV by the German Egyptologist Richard Lepsius (1810–84). Interest in the collection of 'antiquities of the fatherland', encompassing prehistory, early history and the Middle Ages, had also increased since the onset of Romanticism, and that collection likewise required extensive display space.

Idealist aesthetic celebration of classical antiquity had been supplanted by the scholarly, historical approach of modern Classical Studies and Art History, which were according independent value to pre-historic and 'exotic' cultures and to previously disparaged epochs in the history of art. The display of plaster casts in the Neues Museum reflected this change (fig. 55). In the Academy the casts had functioned canonically as a series of classically orientated models for artists. Now, located in the most imposing sequence of galleries on the main floor of the museum, they formed a wide-ranging study collection that chronologically documented the 'progress' of art. Prints and drawings, coins and medals, items from the former *Kunstkammer* and architectural models were stored and exhibited on the top floor – all of them major works of art in their own right, but also a rich collection of source material for cultural and artistic studies. Von Olfers had trained as a scientist, so it was perhaps only natural that he, like Stüler, should aim above all to provide a systematic survey of artistic practice among all peoples of the world at all times.

Seen in the context of this historical and scholarly approach, the Neues Museum emerges as a multi-functional supplementary building whose overriding purpose was the logical arrangement, functional categorisation and expert preservation, presentation and illumination of its exhibits. Stüler promoted this goal by designing a structure of four wings divided in the middle by a fifth to form two courts, the Egyptian and the Greek Court (inside covers and fig. 5). This enabled daylight to enter many galleries from two directions.

The palatial museum, which faces east and west, is slightly asymmetrical because it was originally obstructed by the Levy house (demolished in 1859). Protruding

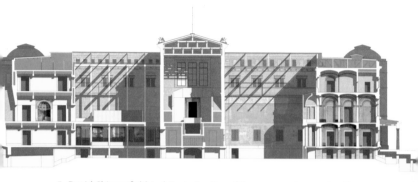

5 David Chipperfield Architects, Section of the proposed reconstruction of the Neues Museum, showing (left to right), the north wing, the Egyptian Court, the Staircase Hall, the Greek Court and the south wing

domed pavilions mark the corners of the eastern façade, while the two longe sides are articulated by a tall central projection with low Greek pediments. Contrasting with the continuous colonnades, these two projections accentuate the area of the building housing the Vestibule and the Staircase Hall, which extends at full height from one side of the structure to the other and ends at the top in an open roof truss (figs. 5, 21). From the moment the visitor enters the building via the main steps it is clear that Stüler, rather like Schinkel with his Pantheon-based rotunda in the Altes Museum, aimed to create an overwhelmingly imposing space that proclaimed and reinforced the intellectual and cultural ideals embodied in the museum.

Stüler, who felt that a building housing works of art should itself be a work of art, turned to the latest models for the Neues Museum. These included Leo von Klenze's New Hermitage in St Petersburg (1839–55), the designs for which Klenze showed the Prussian king in Potsdam in 1840, a meeting undoubtedly attended by Stüler. What has hitherto gone unnoticed is the influence of Klenze's (unexe-

6 Leo von Klenze, View of the proposed royal palace in Athens, detail, 1835, oil on canvas, State Hermitage Museum, St Petersburg

cuted) design for the royal palace in Athens (1834; fig. 6).[1] This is apparent in the proportions of the vertical projections to the horizontals of the body of the structure and in the Doric colonnades. Striking similarity also exists between the windows of three lights that pierce the central projections almost all the way up and culminate in Corinthian orders and, not least, between the late neoclassical formal vocabulary used in both designs (fig. 7). On the other hand, Schinkel's influence is felt in the more vibrant articulation of the mouldings and window apertures in relation to the walls and the planes. And by Stüler's own account, the royal hall that Schinkel included in his design for the palace in Athens (1834) – another unexecuted work, in-

7   The Neues Museum, 1930, east façade

tended for the Acropolis – inspired the Neues Museum's spectacular open roof truss, a feature considered to be typically 'Greek' in contemporary architectural discourse (fig. 42). Klenze promptly adopted it in 1834 for his own Athens palace design and in 1836 made a corresponding change to his plans for the Walhalla near Regensburg. Stüler's version of this architectural 'pathos formula' was undoubtedly the most impressive, not least for its role in the variegated spatial orchestration of the Neues Museum.

The starkness of the exterior has often caused the structure as a whole to be underrated. Yet the interior, for all its clear, functional arrangement, displays a high level of originality and variety in the shaping and decoration of the

8 Section through the north wing, 1862, lithographic reproduction after
Friedrich August Stüler

spaces. A number of technological and structural innova-
tions were rediscovered during preliminary work on the
restoration, prompting historians of art and architecture
to form a far more favourable opinion of the building.
Stüler's section drawings show the relative thinness of the
walls and the filigree-like iron load-bearing and ceiling constructions, features that reduced the overall mass and load
of the building (fig. 8). This was an urgent requirement in
view of the fact that the whole structure rested on pile
foundations in a problematic 'Ice Age swamp pocket'. A re-
duction in mass was also achieved by the revival, in many of
the flat domes and 'Prussian vaults', of an ancient technique
in which the vault consists of a series of terracotta pots

9 Bowstring girders, 1862, lithographic reproduction after Friedrich
August Stüler

(produced in the brick factory of Ernst March, using the
technique employed in 1838 in the reconstruction of the
St Petersburg Hermitage). In his structural analysis of the
building Werner Lorenz has shown that Stüler's spectacular
iron construction just predates that employed by Henri
Labrouste in his well-known library buildings in Paris. On
his travels in Britain in 1826 Schinkel had admired and
sketched the cast-iron supports, beams, ring anchors and
bowstring girders in the factories and spinning mills near
Manchester. At some places in the Neues Museum his pupil
and successor Stüler hid such features, but at others – in
the Room of the Niobids, for example – he exposed them to
view and developed them artistically so as to combine

structural stability with aesthetic elegance (figs. 9, 10). Drawing on the advantages of both cast and wrought iron, these elements were produced serially in the engineering works of August Borsig and then assembled on site. The ornaments of cast zinc and the bronze plating were provided by the factories of Simon Pierre Davranne and Moritz Geiss. What Lorenz calls the 'new, industrial Prussian art of construction' was also apparent in the first use in Germany of steam engines on a building-site railway, which, in combination with a forty-metre-high lift, reduced the time needed for construction by almost a year. And for the first time a steam-operated pile-driver was used to insert wooden piles – more than two thousand of them – into the earth to form the foundations.

The Neues Museum's structural complexity was echoed by its lavish, all-encompassing interior decoration. This was adapted iconographically to the various areas of the collection and to the function of individual spaces, but in its multi-coloured profusion it evinced a distracting *horror vacui*. The architectural theories of Carl Boetticher doubtless played a part in this.[2] In his *Tektonik der Hellenen* (1844/52) Boetticher stated that a structural 'core form' should be clothed in an 'artistic form' in order to distract attention from purely constructional matters and heighten aesthetically the intellectual, spiritual and symbolic purpose of the building. This approach harboured two risks for a museum, regardless of the artistic and technical quality of its decoration. First, there was a danger that exhibits would be overwhelmed by the decoration, a criticism levelled at Klenze's new museums in Munich, the Glyptothek (1816–30) and the Pinakothek (1826–36), and soon to be voiced with regard to the Neues Museum. Second, there might be a tendency to burden museums with ideological baggage in the form of iconographical programmes

HISTORY AND SIGNIFICANCE

10   The Room of the Niobids (2.11.), 2009

based on states of knowledge and *Weltanschauungen* that could rapidly become outdated.

The large-scale murals by the Bavarian court painter Wilhelm von Kaulbach (1805–74) in the Staircase Hall of the Neues Museum are a case in point (1847–66; fig. 41). Among the outstanding works of nineteenth-century German history painting, they were executed at the king's wish in the new 'stereochrome' technique, which imitated the kind of three-dimensional effects possible with oil painting, and they interpreted the collections on display as marking stages in a passage to ever higher levels of cultural development. The view of the world they encapsulate encompasses Hegel's three ages, the Mythological, Classical and Romantic, and is ultimately racially determined, rooted in the perceived victory of Christian Germanic peoples. Corresponding to the six days of Creation described in the Bible, the philosophy of history outlined in the murals comprises six 'turning-points' in the evolution of humanity, beginning with the destruction of the tower of Babel (standing for the separation of races) and ending with Martin Luther and the Reformation (representing the relationship between the individual and God propagated by Protestantism and the desire for an independent German nation).[3]

Murals also decorated the galleries, to 'establish a place for living art and to grant it appropriate surroundings in which to speak and develop', as Stüler put it. The aim was not only to make the museum a total work of art, but also to provide didactic pictorial commentaries and furnish exhibits with historically apt contexts. Thus the Egyptian Court, a 380-square-metre space spanned by a glass ceiling without supports and containing an imposing columned ambulatory, is a reconstruction of the Ramesseum in Thebes (the funerary temple of Ramses II, 1290–24 BC) at a third of the original size (fig. 11). In the murals the painter–brothers Ernst and

11 The Egyptian Court, 1862, lithographic reproduction according to a design by Eduard Gaertner

Max Weidenbach collaborated with the architect Georg Gustav Erbkam, who had taken part in the excavations in Egypt, to create idealised pictorial reconstructions of Egyptian sites and buildings (fig. 12). Wall paintings in the room devoted to 'antiquities of the fatherland' epitomised Germanic cultural topography through images of the Stubbenkammer promontory and a megalithic grave on the island of Rügen, while a cycle of eleven murals (partly preserved) depicted for the first time in German art a wide range of Nordic deities as recorded in the thirteenth-century *Eddas* (figs. 34, 36). Stüler

12 Karl Eduard Biermann, *The Island of Philae*, mural in the Egyptian
Court (1.12.), photographed in 2009

also provided an appropriate didactic setting for the collection of plaster casts, encompassing works from classical antiquity to the modern era and housed in galleries on the
main floor. He himself chose the idealised views of Greek and
Roman buildings, cities and landscapes that appeared on the
walls alongside a selection of mythological scenes (figs. 50–
52). Subjects from the imperial history of the Christian West
decorated the medieval galleries, while allegories of the arts
and technology (including machine production) supple-
mented the display in the Modern Room.

This presentation of cultural history soon clashed not
only with developments in knowledge and general atti-

HISTORY AND SIGNIFICANCE

tudes, but also with the growing size of the collections, changes in display strategies and the dynamics of a modern museum. Stüler's architecture, structurally and aesthetically outstanding, and the historicist orientation of the displays it housed, including the murals, unquestionably offer impressive artistic testimony to the state of scholarly endeavour and human knowledge at the time of their creation. Yet by the 1880s both were being criticised because they made it difficult for the collections to keep step with the changing times. A series of radical alterations in the museum's contents, for instance, began only two decades after the opening, including the transfer of the objects from the *Kunstkammer* to the new Kunstgewerbemuseum, of the ethnographical collection to the Völkerkundemuseum and, after the First World War, of the plaster casts to the Berlin university. The 1920s and 1930s saw a partial rearrangement of the holdings and a modernisation of the museum that entailed remodelling certain sections. These developments caused some wall decorations to be covered and some galleries to be 'neutralised'.

BOMB DAMAGE AND REBUILDING PLANS, 1945–2003

The Neues Museum was closed at the outbreak of the Second World War in 1939 and its contents removed to safety. It suffered severe bomb damage in 1943–45. After eight decades as a museum, it now embarked on a fifty-year period as a ruin with nothing but makeshift protection against further decay. The Staircase Hall had been completely gutted. Nothing survived of the north-west wing, two adjacent sides of the Egyptian Court, the south-east projection with its domed space and roughly one third of the interior decoration. The roofing, most galleries and interior surfaces, the

13 The Staircase Hall, 1985, looking east

building's outer shell, the Greek Court, the architectural orna-
ment and the area outside with its pergolas had all sustained severe damage. Protective measures carried out in
the 1980s involved the removal of some sections and the
destruction of further architectural and sculptural remains
(figs. 13, 14). Plans for rebuilding were long doomed to failure, not least because the state conservation authority in
the German Democratic Republic had decided that the entire museum should be reconstructed in its original state,
including the murals by Kaulbach. In 1986 East German cultural politicians eventually agreed on a restoration of the
prestigious building at a cost of 350 million marks as part of

HISTORY AND SIGNIFICANCE

14 The Neues Museum, *c.* 1985, west façade

a 'Programme of Development for the Capital of the GDR'. Shortly after work commenced in September 1989, the peaceful revolution and the fall of the Berlin Wall led to a new political era in eastern Germany.

After 1990 German reunification not only brought together collections previously divided between East and West Berlin, but also led to an intensive debate among those responsible in both parts of the city about the future of Berlin's museums, and the Museum Island in particular. The Stiftung Preußischer Kulturbesitz, acting on a proposal of its Committee for Architectural Monuments, appointed a mixed committee of experts to investigate the case of the Neues Museum. Chaired by Wolfgang Wolters, the committee sat in 1991 and 1992 and revised some crucial aspects of the plans drawn up in the GDR.[4] Rejecting complete reconstruction of the original building as unacceptable in conservational, museological and artistic terms, it based its recommendations on the 1964 International Charter for the Conservation and Restoration of Monuments and Sites (the 'Venice Charter'). The committee proposed that existing parts of the original building, including elements recovered from elsewhere, be conserved carefully and, if necessary, partly restored, with the greatest respect for their value as authentic historical documents. It further proposed that sensitive modern additions be made in order to render the ruin a structurally intact unit suitable for use as a museum. The aim should be to generate not the romantic sentiment associated with ruins, but an experience of the building's original aura and the high quality of its detailing. An 'augmented rebuilding' should reflect the historicity of the Neues Museum, but also make visible its ageing and the damage it had incurred, rather than grant it a false 'new splendour'. The experts were convinced that a reconstruction of the original surfaces, however meticulous, could only result in fictions that would undermine the value of the surviving sections to such an extent as to support Georg Mörsch's claim that reconstruction would amount to a 'second destruction'.

In 1992 the Berlin conservation authority, the Landesamt für Denkmalpflege,[5] adopted the recommendations of the expert committee in the form of an 'outline conservation plan' and promoted them vigorously in difficult negotiations with the Stiftung Preußischer Kulturbesitz, which, as the building's user, was pursuing a different line. In 1993, after the committee had submitted its initial recommendations,

HISTORY AND SIGNIFICANCE

the Stiftung announced a competition for the reconstruction of the Neues Museum in combination with a new building. The competition terms were far less restrictively worded than the committee's recommendations: 'Solutions to the task should not be limited to the restoration and reconstruction of the original building. The competition organiser expects that the possibilities opened up by the term "augmented rebuilding" in the conservation commission's recommendations will be used to balance conservation interests with the functional concerns of the museum.' The goal here was a modernisation that was not only technical, but also museological and aesthetic, one that took into account the needs and expectations of modern museum tourism – gallery arrangements that permit visitors to focus on highlights, for example, or that facilitate up-to-date 'stagings' of artistic treasures (fig. 15). The effect of this recommendation was to polarize the preservationist and museological positions, and led in the following years to the publicly conducted 'Berlin museum dispute'.

In 1994 the Italian architect Giorgio Grassi was proclaimed winner of the competition. His proposed substitutes for the missing sections of the Neues Museum were couched in a rigorously rationalist mode. Stüler's Staircase Hall was to become a three-storey exhibition space, linked at ground level with a new building standing next to the Kupfergraben. Second prize in the competition went to David Chipperfield, the only participant who met conservation demands for a restoration of the Neues Museum, including the Staircase Hall. Despite subsequent claims by disappointed critics, at no point did Chipperfield state that he intended to restore the original building *in toto*. Rather, in full accord with the expert committee's recommendations he proposed that 'this restoration should be as complete and as authentic as possible', an idea he later put into practice. Chipperfield's highly controversial steel-and-glass proposal for the new building beside the Kupfergraben contrasted starkly with his close adherence to the historical modes of construction and the original form of the surviving sections of the museum. The third prize-winner, Francesco Venezia of Naples, rejected an 'augmented rebuilding' of the Neues Museum completely. His designs, along with those of Axel Schulte, who received fifth prize, did not figure in subsequent developments.

However, the fourth prize-winner, Frank Gehry, had submitted a proposal that gained increasing favour with the Stiftung. A sequence of deconstructivist metal structures on stilts was to wind its way along the Kupfergraben at the edge of the Lustgarten, beginning at the west façade of the Schinkel museum, crossing the Bodestraße and continuing to the glazed hall of the Pergamon Museum. Gehry planned to restore the exterior of the Neues Museum, but to remodel the interior completely, regardless of the surviving parts. The jury censured his proposal because 'the individual masses were highly autonomous in appearance and articulation and ignored the existing typology of the city'. Yet the creation of such utterly distinctive buildings is this architect's hallmark, the source of the 'Bilbao effect' – a term describing how the spectacular architecture of a single museum building by Gehry has sufficed to attract thousands of tourists to the Basque city every year. Some museum administrators in Berlin hoped that Gehry's visionary plan would prove to be a liberating blow, catapulting the Museum Island into the twenty-first century. The Stiftung requested the prize-winners to revise their entries, but in a third round eliminated Grassi and concentrated on Chipperfield and Gehry, requesting them in spring 1997 to produce new versions of their proposals. A clear preference for Gehry began to emerge. This prompted intensive

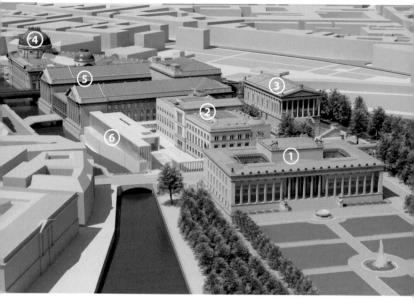

15 The master plan for the Museum Island, 2006, computer rendering by David Chipperfield Architects (1: Altes Museum, 1830; 2: Neues Museum, 1859; 3: Alte Nationalgalerie, 1876; 4: Bode Museum, 1904; 5: Pergamon Museum, 1930; 6: James Simon Gallery, construction scheduled to begin in 2010)

action on the part of the Berlin conservation authorities, several other expert bodies (including the national conservation association, the Vereinigung der Landesdenkmalpfleger der Bundesrepublik Deutschland), specialists, journalists and members of the public. In public debates, press reports and resolutions they all vociferously demanded the enforcement of conservation principles. The local conservation council, the Landesdenkmalrat, held a press conference in November 1997, immediately before the final decision was due to be taken by the Stiftung's committee in the Berlin parliament. This helped to tip the balance in favour of Chipperfield, whose proposal promised a successful balance of conservation and modernisation requirements.

THE CHIPPERFIELD/HARRAP CONSERVATION PHILOSOPHY

The tensions of autumn 1997 relaxed once the commission had been awarded. There ensued a period of constructive discussion and close cooperation among everyone concerned, under the aegis of Klaus-Dieter Lehmann, president of the Stiftung, Peter-Klaus Schuster, director general of state museums in Berlin, and Gisela Holan, head of the Stiftung's building department. Henceforth, the architects, conservation professionals and museum directors consulted the Bundesamt für Bauwesen und Raumordnung,[6] part of the federal body with final responsibility for all building activity, to achieve consensus on the complex problems and measures involved in the reconstruction, each and every one of which required an individual solution.

David Chipperfield, Julian Harrap and their staff[7] shared with the expert committee, the local conservation authority (which in 2000 drew up a detailed restoration plan) and the client the overriding aim of preserving and repairing the original fabric of the building as far as possible. Their approach to historic monuments rested – and rests – on two ethical foundations: the writings of John Ruskin (1819–1900), the English father of modern conservation, whose ideas prompted the meticulous conservation practice customary in Britain (and for a long time standard procedure in the treatment of archaeological remains from classical antiquity), and the post-war West German tradition (as represented by the architect Hans Döllgast and others) of keeping damage visible, repairing it only minimally and adapting it to new requirements. Carlo Scarpa's new interpretations of historic buildings through bold additions to their original substance should also be cited in this context, especially his museum projects in Italy in the 1950s and 1960s.

Appropriate solutions to the various problems were aided by a series of record books in which the state of preservation of each space in the museum was recorded exactly and analysed. The complexity of the conservation and restoration measures, some of them devised specially and tested beforehand, was determined on the basis of these books and in relation to the degree of damage in each space.[8] Replacements and additions were distinguished clearly from the originals, as stipulated in the Venice Charter. The building fabric remains visible in places because it was decided not to cover the walls and other surfaces with new layers of plaster or paint. By revealing lower layers, these 'naked' areas offer glimpses of the building's construction.

Yet surviving sections conserved with archaeological exactitude would not be allowed to inhabit a wholly neutral context: to refurbish fragments in a way that precluded aesthetic consonance with their surroundings could not be countenanced in a functional work of architecture of this quality and importance. 'The building "wants" to be a building again', Chipperfield wrote in 2003: he wished to restore order to the whole and significance to the parts. The task, then, was both to reformulate the unity of each space, as defined by its shape, construction, supports, vaulting system, cycles of paintings, ornaments and state of preservation, and once more to make sense of the sequence of galleries as a continuum. This meant devising an individual architectural vocabulary that would both suit the new spaces and facilitate restrained stylised additions to the surviving historical sections. Conservation issues thus automatically became design issues: 'It has been our ambition to bind these two activities into a single approach, the new and the old reinforcing each other, not in a desire for contrast, but in a search for continuity.'

The logic of the 'augmented rebuilding' approach excluded fulfilment of some widespread wishes. These included two 'inconsistent' demands – for a meticulous reconstruction of the historical exterior skin of the building in combination with the creation of modern sequences of galleries inside, and for a precise reconstruction of certain individual spaces – the Staircase Hall, for instance – in combination with an eschewal of reproductions of this kind elsewhere. Such proposals, apart from lacking any intellectual or methodological foundation, would have encouraged similar arbitrariness in other areas. To promote a true historical and architectural understanding of Stüler's museum in its surviving form it was necessary to make the interaction between original sections and additions as clearly visible as possible throughout the building. That also held for the interior decoration, with the status quo functioning as the point of reference.

Chipperfield himself did not shy away from 'inconsistent' interventions if the artistic and historical circumstances justified them. For example, acting on a suggestion made by conservation experts, he constructed a stylised version of the exedra that had been removed from the Greek Court during a remodelling undertaken in 1919–23 for the Amarna collection (fig. 16). The rationale here was that the exedra had been an important spatial component of the original flat-domed Medieval Room. Another instance of 'inconsistency' concerned the asymmetrical groin vault in the neo-Gothic Star Room on the top floor. Stüler

HISTORY AND SIGNIFICANCE

16 The Medieval Room (2.04.), 2009, view of the niche

had fitted this Rabitz construction (the first plaster and wire
mesh ceiling in Germany) into the south-west corner to
create an atmosphere appropriate to the display of precious objects from the *Kunstkammer*. Only a few remnants
of the original survived, but the curiosity value of the vault
decided the debate over complete 'purification' versus
complete reconstruction in favour of the latter (fig. 60). Similarly, the mosaics (whose *tesserae* had been recovered in
the post-war years and packed almost to overflowing in
Russian ammunition crates) and the terrazzo floors (which

had been destroyed entirely) were reconstructed wherever the rhythm of the columns justified this procedure in terms of continuity between galleries and structural clarity – in the Modern Room, for instance (figs. 34, 54, 56). Despite such occasional breaches of strict conservation principles, Chipperfield's 'augmented rebuilding' of the Neues Museum is largely transparent to the observant visitor.

ACCESS, SERVICING AND HIGH TECH

New functional and technical standards and norms had to be incorporated into the reconstructed museum if it was to satisfy the latest requirements. The difficulty of implementing such demands without sacrificing aesthetic integrity are often overlooked. From 1989 to 1994, for instance, the rotting wooden foundation grille of the Neues Museum was replaced by 2,500 steel microbore piles and a new foundation plate, subsequently adapted to changes in planning. Further examples are the strengthening of the load-bearing capacity of the historical iron supports by means of carbon fibre slats and the refurbishment of all the windows to meet current thermal insulation standards.

In 1999, while the master plan for the Museum Island was being drawn up, it was decided that the Neues Museum should once more house the Egyptian and the pre- and early history collections. Fortunately, this meant that the old main entrances could be retained. On the other hand, the bridges that had linked the Neues Museum with the Altes Museum in the south since 1845, and with the Pergamon Museum in the north since 1925, were not to be reconstructed, not least because they could not have accommodated the anticipated masses of visitors and

17 David Chipperfield Architects, Proposal for the James Simon Gallery
and the Neues Museum, 2006

would have made any rearrangement of the collections
inside the building more difficult. The master plan replaced the bridges by an 'Archaeological Promenade'
(figs. 15, 19, 29). Beginning at a new entrance structure on
the Kupfergraben, this would form a below-ground con-
nection between the individual buildings and their exhibition areas, including basements and courts and providing
space for displays devoted to such general aspects of cultural history as 'Gott und Götter' (God and Gods), 'Chaos
und Kosmos' (Chaos and the Cosmos), 'Zeit und Geschichte' (Time and History) and 'Jenseits und Ewigkeit' (The Be-

18 Central controls of the heating and air-conditioning system, 2009

yond and Eternity). This solution catered both for concen-
trations of tourist groups visiting the main attractions of
the various museums and for individual visitors staying
for longer periods of time.

Chipperfield's revised design for the entrance to the Archaeological Promenade adhered to the principle that every
building on the Museum Island should reflect stylistically
the period of its construction. Though 'modern', the revision
took into account criticisms levelled at the first proposal for
its radical formal vocabulary and materials. This new James
Simon Gallery was better accommodated to the urban fabric as a whole, echoing Stüler's system of colonnades to
evoke classical articulation and employing polymer con-

HISTORY AND SIGNIFICANCE

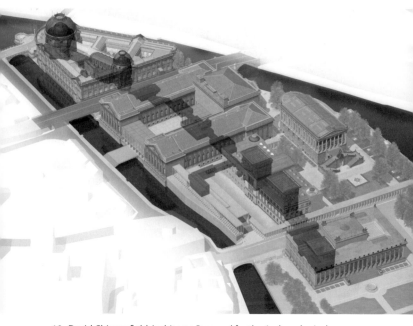

19 David Chipperfield Architects, Proposal for the Archaeological
Promenade, 2006

crete to approximate natural stone (fig. 17). Construction is
scheduled to begin in 2010.

The Archaeological Promenade precluded the use of the
Neues Museum's basement storey as an inconspicuous
home for security, energy, transportation, air-conditioning
and lighting facilities that met modern high tech requirements. The central controls of these facilities have therefore
been housed in below-ground spaces to the east of the
building and beneath the roofs. Considerable ingenuity was
required to install the new technical infrastructure in the
heating and service shafts of the old building (most up-to-
date in their day), in the monopitched roofs of the colonnades and in the cavities above the barrel vaults in such a

way that they remained invisible from the outside. This un-
obtrusive technological upgrading is one of the outstanding
planning and engineering achievements of the reconstruction (fig. 18).

GUIDED TOUR

THE EXTERIOR

Visitors approaching the Neues Museum from the Perga-mon Museum or the Zeughaus see the rear façade, which faces west. Its central projection and south wing (on the right) have been carefully restored, whereas the north wing is clearly a new structure (fig. 1). The horizontal mouldings and the windows of this new wing echo the main lines of the old building, while the colour of the bricks, made in long-established Brandenburg brick factories, approximates that of the older sections. Remains of plaster, imitating various kinds of dressed stone, appear in the south wing, which retains the original sculpted figures in the window mullions. By contrast, the window bars in the north, light in colour and square in cross-section, stand out from their surroundings so as to grant the new wing approximately the same visual weight as its old counterpart. When the James Simon Gallery has been completed, only the upper third of the west façade will be visible, as it had been until about 1935, when Schinkel's Packhof building was demolished entirely (fig. 17).

20 The Neues Museum, 2009, west façade, upper section of
the central projection

The upper section of the west façade's central projection, pierced vertically by two tripartite windows, has been
reconstructed. August Kiss's sculptures in the pediment, dating from 1856 and cast in zinc in imitation of stone, depict
'Art instructing Industry and the Arts and Crafts' and thus
allude to one of the museum's most important functions.
The inscription beneath the pediment, chosen by King
Friedrich Wilhelm IV, reads 'Artem non odit nisi ignarus' (Only
the ignorant despise art) and underscores the museum's éli-
tist didactic aims (fig. 20).

21   David Chipperfield Architects, Proposal for the Neues Museum, east façade, 2006

The Neues Museum's front façade, facing the Alte Nationalgalerie in the east, had survived apart from the southeast corner pavilion and presents a more unified appearance than its western counterpart. Its pedestal is formed by the continous columned pergola at its base. As in the rear façade, the main storey and the far lower top floor are linked visually by the strong verticals of the central projection. The notably clear-cut window mouldings on both levels betray Stüler's rigorous hand. In this façade, too, no attempt has been made to disguise war damage, but the whole does appear more or less homogeneous. This effect was increased by the reinstatement in 1990 of the dome on the north-east pavilion. Its new pendant in the south corner, however, contrasts quite sharply with the rest of the façade. The three figures let into the exposed brick on the east face of the south pavilion echo the sculptures and medallions depicting the arts and sciences that have been reinstalled in a similar position in the north pavilion (figs. 7, 21, 22). The pediment of the central projection, its sculptures designed by Friedrich Drake and once crowned by a figure of Borussia (a female personification of Prussia), contains a carefully restored stucco relief showing 'History instructing Architecture, Sculpture, Painting and Drawing'[9] – an indication of the new approach to museums in the historicist period. Beneath this appears the inscription 'Museum a patre beatissimo conditum ampliavit filius MDCCCLV' (The museum founded by the most blessed father was expanded by the son, 1855). Cast-zinc allegorical *genii* decorate the window mullions, their attributes alluding to the fields covered by the collections.

THE VESTIBULE
AND NORTH TOUR

Passing through the doors, visitors enter the rigorously designed Vestibule (1.01.), its four monumental Doric columns bearing a coffered ceiling of terracotta pots arranged between cast-iron bending supports. In formal terms the space resembles the well-known Greek Vestibule of Schinkel's Humboldt palace in Tegel (1819–24). Most columns in the museum consist of blank shafts stuccoed with marble cement, but those in the Vestibule are carefully fluted monoliths of white Carrara marble with veins of dark violet. In the Roman manner, the capitals bear friezes, and the columns therefore evoke the transition from ancient Greek to ancient Roman architecture (fig. 23). As in Leo von Klenze's New Hermitage in St Petersburg, a single flight of stairs ascends from the Vestibule's central bay into the Staircase Hall. The walls of the Vestibule are faced with polished, pale yellow imitation marble (*stucco lustro*). Replacing destroyed original sculptures, replicas of the Antique Egyptian-style lions from the Capitol steps in Rome stand on plinths at either side of the foot of the stairs. The replicas (1875) come from the former Universum exhibition grounds near the Lehrter Stadtbahnhof in Berlin. From

22 The Neues Museum, 2009, south façade

23 The Vestibule (1.01.), 2009

the Vestibule, the south tour begins on the left with the Fatherland Room (Vaterländischer Saal). On the right, visitors enter the Mythological Room (Mythologischer Saal), housing part of the Egyptian collection.

Large sections of precious blue-and-gold painted paper were uncovered and restored in the Mythological Room (1.11.), which is articulated by wall piers (figs. 24, 25). They appear on the ceiling and on the cross-beams masking the iron bowstring girders. Their astrological imagery includes copies of the zodiac from the temple of Dendera, made by

24 The Mythological Room (1.11.), 2009

Richard Lepsius in the Louvre in Paris. Damage to the decoration in this room resulted from modernisation measures implemented in the 1930s, which involved inserting a false ceiling and wiping off or covering the historical decoration. One of the circulating friezes depicts aspects of the Egyptian cult of the dead, another the chief gods of Egyptian mythology. The lower sections of the walls bear painting that imitates wooden panelling, complete with the wood grain. Mummies, sarcophagi and burial offerings were displayed in the Mythological Room. The adjacent Tomb Room (Grä-

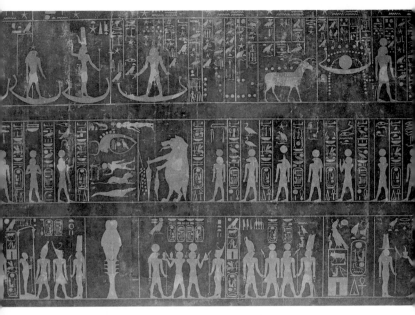

25 The Mythological Room (1.11.), 2009, detail of the ceiling paper

bersaal, 1.10.), an almost perfectly square space beneath the
North Dome Room (Nordkuppelsaal), contained three accessible tomb chambers from Gizeh and Sakkara, parts of
which were not uncovered until measures were carried out
to protect the derelict museum (the chambers are now installed in the Historical Room).

The former Hypostyle (Hypostyl, 1.09.) forms part of the
new north-west section of the museum. Its exhibits included a cast of the Rosetta Stone (British Museum, London),
whose multilingual inscriptions helped Jean-François Cham-
pollion to decipher hieroglyphic writing in 1822. Today, the
Hypostyle is articulated by wall panels of polymer concrete
and stele-like glass cases designed by Michele de Lucchi.

26 View from the Historical Room (1.08) into the Egyptian Court, 2009

From here visitors can enter the room of the redesigned Egyptian Court.

The north tour continues with the Historical Room (Historischer Saal, 1.08.), once elaborately decorated, but now rebuilt as a modern exhibition area in the old format yet without the original columns. Like most new sections of the museum, it is articulated by means of finely polished or sandblasted pre-cast concrete elements and by ceilings with beams. The inclusion of Saxon marble chips in the white cement mix, couched in warm shades of grey, gives the impression that the large blocks are made from modern artificial marble (fig. 26). Chipperfield devised a puristic formal vocabulary for these elements that also proved eminently suitable for sections of the building where new meets old. The north tour ends in a space behind the stairs, which has been redesigned as a vestibule for the new west entrance (1.07.).

THE EGYPTIAN COURT

As described above, the north tour skirts three sides of the Egyptian Court (1.12.), which originally contained one of the museum's most spectacular displays. Eduard Gaertner's striking chromolithograph of the Egyptian Court stills governs our notions of the Egyptian section in Berlin today (1862; figs. 8, 11). The court was conceived from the outset as an interior exhibition space, with a 360-square-metre ceiling of frosted glass – the first of its kind and size in Berlin – suspended from the glass pitched roof. All that remained after the museum ruin had been secured were the south and east sides (with fragments of wall paintings) and some shaped stones (rescued in 1987) from the sixteen Egyptian columns and their lotus capitals. The original frieze bore a hieroglyphic dedication to King Friedrich Wilhelm IV, intelligible only to the initiated, that lauded him as the 'victorious lord of the Rhine and the Weichsel', the patron of the Egyptian expedition and the founder of the Egyptian Museum. The polychrome peristyle, containing statues of pharaohs and deities, surrounded an atrium three steps down and was designed in imitation of the Ramesseum in Thebes. On all four sides the peristyle supported a gallery with casts of Egyptian, Assyrian, Persian and ancient Greek works. In 1992 the expert committee judged the Egyptian Court an almost completely irretrievable loss (fig. 14). Its lamentable condition prompted a radically new solution.

27   David Chipperfield Architects, Proposal for the Egyptian Court

Chipperfield's design inverted space and mass (fig. 27). He replaced the open atrium by a structure-within-a-structure inserted into the court with open space on all sides. This display platform encompasses two-storeys, its simple forms constructed from polymer concrete and matted glass. The choice of formal vocabulary was certainly not without significance. It brings to mind Friedrich Gilly's sketches of Egyptian columned structures (*c.* 1796; fig. 28), which possessed great importance for Schinkel and the pioneers of twentieth-century architectural modernism. In addition, the architectural theorists of Romantic neoclassicism accorded the hypostyle halls of Thebes and Karnak a major historical role as the cra-

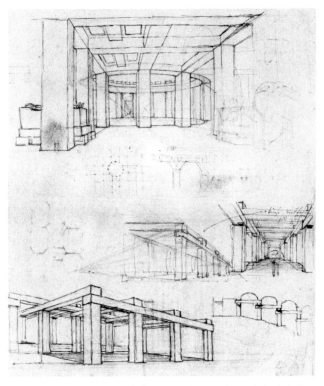

28 Friedrich Gilly, Columned halls, *c.* 1796, drawing, formerly Technische Hochschule, Charlottenburg, Berlin (whereabouts unknown)

dle of 'Greco-Germanic building'. Finally, Chipperfield himself had been profoundly affected by the Egyptian originals. The Romantic aura of his new Egyptian Court is enhanced by the way the floor of the former atrium has been opened to provide access to the vault-like space of the Archaeological Promenade on the basement floor (0.12.), where Egyptian and Antique stone sarcophagi illustrate the theme of 'Jenseits und Ewigkeit' (The Beyond and Eternity). From this vantage point, the space also opens up in the opposite di-

29 The Egyptian Court (1.12.), including part of the Archaeological Promenade (0.12.), 2009

rection, offering a striking view up into the court with its roof of satin-finished glass.

Pompeii-style murals by Carl Graeb, Wilhelm Schirmer, Eduard Pape, Eduard Biermann and Max Schmidt originally decorated the walls of the gallery in the Egyptian Court (1.12.). They depicted sites visited by Lepsius on his Egyptian expedition along with visual reconstructions of the relevant archaeological monuments. The surviving paintings in this instructive cycle give a good idea of its qualities: on the east wall, views of the obelisk in the temple of Karnak, the forecourt of the temple of Edfu, the island of Philae, the rock temple of Abu Simbel and Mount Barkal; on the north wall,

30　The Ethnographical Room (1.06.), 2009

remnants of a view of the stone quarries at Gebel el-Silsila (figs. 12, 29).[10] All other sections of these walls show exposed brickwork, while the new walls in the south and west echo this archaeological character through the use of old bricks from Brandenburg.

SOUTH TOUR

From the rear vestibule (1.07.) visitors move south into the former Ethnographical Room (Ethnographischer Saal, 1.06.). This long space, articulated by six pairs of Doric columns and

31 The Flat Dome Room (1.04.), 2008

lit from the west, originally housed art produced by 'the kind of wholly barbaric peoples encountered in Africa and Oceania', the objects that later formed the nucleus of the Museum für Völkerkunde. Variations in the state of preservation of the Doric marble-cement fluting added to the sandstone column shafts are clearly visible. This contrasts with the fully restored terrazzo floor. The conjunction of the two results in what Georg Mörsch has termed an 'equilibrium that makes visible both the form and the passage of time' (fig. 30).

From the end of the Ethnographical Room, on the left, visitors pass into the Flat Dome Room (Flachkuppelsaal,

1.04.), once reserved for what a description of 1855 calls the 'more significant objects' produced in Polynesia and India. The original nine bays were reduced to six during a 1920s remodelling. Columns and pilasters support flat domes featuring the terracotta pot construction typical of Stüler. Their elaborate, elegant ornamentation has survived largely intact (fig. 31). The narrow space separated from the Flat Dome Room by a wall in the south now houses the museum café (1.05.). A new, columned exedra reintroduces a northern extension to the Flat Dome Room and offers an excellent view of the Greek Court.

THE GREEK COURT
AND THE SCHIEVELBEIN FRIEZE

The exedra in the Flat Dome Room is a good vantage point from which to view the Greek Court (Griechischer Hof, 0.13.; fig. 32). Like the Egyptian Court in the north, the Greek Court helped to light the adjacent galleries and, from the remodelling of 1919–23, acted as a covered exhibition space for items from the Amarna excavations. Today, it forms part of the Archaeological Promenade. The fact that it was not originally intended as a display area explains why it possesses the character of an exterior more than its northern counterpart. Despite the survival of fairly large sections of sandstone-coloured plaster with incised markings imitating blocks of dressed stone, the walls and the exedra now achieve their effect principally through the warm tones of the exposed brick fabric. The height of the court was increased by a half-storey from 1883 to 1887, when the monopitched roof, switched to slope outwards instead of inwards, was raised on the inside. Three medallions with the heads of the Greek deities Zeus, Hera and Athena that decorate the outer wall of the

32 The Greek Court (0.13.), 2008, view of north wall

Staircase Hall are visible through the court's new glass roof.

The most significant decorative element in the Greek Court is the Schievelbein frieze, a fine view of which can be had from the exedra of the Flat Dome Room. Named after its creator, Hermann Schievelbein (1817–67), a leading rep-

33 The Greek Court (0.13.), 2009, detail of the Schievelbein frieze, showing Stüler and Olfers welcoming the inhabitants of Pompeii

resentative of neoclassical sculpture in Berlin, the frieze
marks an important stage in the history of museum iconography. In 1845 Schievelbein was commissioned to depict the
destruction of Pompeii and its consequences. Pompeii and
Herculaneum, both cities destroyed by an eruption of Vesuvius in the first century AD, had been rediscovered in the
eighteenth century by archaeologists and travellers. The material brought to light by excavations, and the resulting pub-
lications, henceforth determined notions of refined domes-
tic culture in ancient Rome, not only inspiring the decorative systems of neoclassicism and historicism, but also
prompting the development of modern applied art and its
various techniques. Schievelbein's limestone stucco frieze,
restored in several stages between 1997 and 2008, shows
the destruction of Pompeii by the allegorically rendered
forces of nature (centre of the north wall),[11] the (fictional)
flight of its inhabitants (east wall) and their arrival in Berlin,
where they and their artistic treasures are graciously re-

ceived by the director general of the Berlin museums, von Olfers, and the architect of the Neues Museum, Stüler (west wall; fig. 33). This rather fanciful allegory, showing how vanished cultures survive in modern museums, is still not entirely without relevance.

CONTINUATION OF THE SOUTH TOUR

From the Flat Dome Room (1.04.) visitors pass through the entirely new south-east pavilion and turn left into the Fatherland Room (Vaterländischer Saal, 1.02.), a high point in the original iconography of the museum. This room, subdivided by three pairs of Doric columns bearing segmental arches, housed objects dating from the prehistory and early history of the northern countries. Murals on subjects derived from German legend and the Nordic sagas as recorded in the medieval *Eddas* were painted around the tops of the walls from 1850 to 1852 in order to provide an appropriate framework for the exhibits (figs. 34, 36).[12] These images, which for the first time put Norse mythology on an equal footing with its Greek counterpart, fulfilled a didactic purpose, since few people at the time were familiar with the complex world of the northern gods.* Already disfigured by

---

* The following images survive in part: (west wall, from south to north) the earth mother Hertha in her cart, Day and Night, and All-father Odin with the ravens Hugin and Munin; Baldur, his death as a result of Loki's trickery and, on the right, the goddess Holda's spinning distaff; Freyr, the god of spring, on his boar, dwarfs building the ship Skidbladnir and Freyr's sister Freya in her cat-driven chariot; the valkyries during battle and their ride to Valhalla, under the command of Tyr, the god of war; (on the east wall, from north to south) Hela, goddess of the underworld, the dragon Nidhöggr and Loki, Hela's wicked father, in Niflheim; the three norns with the world ash tree Yggdrasil, the thread of life and the shield inscribed with the deeds of humankind; the water sprites, the treasure guarded by a griffin and the giants' battle with the dragon; dancing elves bearing their queen while Thor (or Donar) sets out in his goat-drawn chariot to do battle with mountain trolls.

34 The Fatherland Room (1.02.), 2009

1900, they were covered completely shortly thereafter and did not come to light again until the conservation of the museum building. The two programmatic landscapes by Ferdinand Konrad Bellermann at the entrance to the room, depicting the Stubbenkammer promontory on Rügen and the island's Arkona temple with a megalithic grave, were re-covered from the rubble of the original south-east pavilion

35 Ferdinand Konrad Bellermann, *Sacrificial Stone near the Stubben-kammer on the Island of Rügen*, mural in the Fatherland Room (1.02.), photographed in 2009

and mounted on its new walls (fig. 35). They continue the Romantic tradition of historically based images of the North as represented by Caspar David Friedrich and Karl Friedrich Schinkel, but in their topographical realism they also form a pendant to the views of Egypt and the Antique world that decorate the Egyptian Court, the Greek Court and the Roman Room. Three lunette-shaped murals on the south wall illustrate the chronology of northern prehistory by Stone and Iron Age rulers' tombs and by a treasure of characteristic bronze and gold burial offerings. On the left, the frieze on the north wall depicts Valhalla, the Norse heaven, with feasting gods and heroes, and, on the right, the path to Helheim, the underworld occupied by all the dead who have not fallen in battle. The Norse All-father in the centre, holding tablets bearing the runes for Salvation and Peace, deliberately resembles the biblical Moses with the tablets of the

36 Gustav Richter, *Valhalla, All-father and the Underworld Helheim*, 'stereochromatic' mural in the Fatherland Room (1.02.), photographed in 2009

law and to the God the Father of Christianity. In other words, the 'twilight of the Germanic gods' would be followed in the evolution of humankind by the dawn of new and greater age, the Christian age of peace (figs. 34, 36).

THE STAIRCASE HALL

The centrepiece of the Neues Museum is still the monumental Staircase Hall ranging over the full height and width of the building (2.00.). Its original function as a mood-setting space embodying a specific philosophy of history has already been outlined. Stüler's primary architectural instrument was a theatrical *mise en scène* of a strictly regular arrangement of stairs. These led on the main floor to an Ionic columned hall inspired by the Erechtheion on the Acropolis in Athens, whence visitors could turn right into the Greek Room or left into the Modern Room (fig. 37). The full dimensions of the Staircase Hall first become apparent when visitors turn around at the top of the first flight of steps to face in the direction they have come. Only then do they see the two flights of steps rising parallel to each other along the side walls, turning towards one another at the top storey and ending in a central landing (fig. 39).

GUIDED TOUR

Light enters the Staircase Hall through the tripartite windows at either end, yet, judging by early photographs, the overall effect was originally rather dark (see back cover). The polychrome splendour of the structure emerged in a precisely orchestrated crescendo as visitors ascended the stairs (figs. 40, 41). From the shadowy austerity of the Doric Vestibule, they passed a cast of the Lion Gate relief from Mycenae (1300 BC) as they walked up the steps of grey Silesian marble, progressing symbolically from the 'primitive' world of Egypt, Oceania and other ancient cultures to the higher realms of classical antiquity and the modern era as reflected in the splendour of the upper hall, with its staircase of yellow and white marble and its noble architectural articulation. Casts of the colossal Roman horse-tamers from the Quirinal in Rome stood in front of the balustrades, while the walls and roof truss were coloured a darkly glowing red à la Pompeii. On the upper landing, in front of the windows, stood a polychrome, scaled-down replica of the caryatid porch from the Erechtheion in Athens (fifth century BC). Friedrich Drake produced the replica, completing the missing sections on the basis of the original Caryatid C in the British Museum, London. Remains of his porch were demolished during measures carried out to save the derelict museum (fig. 13). Column substitutes in the shape of a human body – specifically, a draped female figure –

37 The Staircase Hall (2.00.), 2009, looking west

38 The Staircase Hall (2.00.), 2009, looking south

were an extremely widespread feature of Prussian late neo-classicism in the mid-nineteenth century. Contemporary theories of art, for example Friedrich Wilhelm von Schelling's aesthetics, saw in them the epitome of the ancient Greeks' fundamentally anthropomorphic approach to art. Ultimately, however, the Greeks' anthropomorphism was deemed 'heathen', subsequently transcended by the notion of humankind espoused by the Christian West – the rise of which was depicted in Wilhelm von Kaulbach's history paintings on the walls of the Staircase Hall. The open roof truss, a feature derived from Schinkel, embodied a marriage of the Antique and the Christian ideals (fig. 42). This kind of wooden truss, with its panthers, deer, lions, griffins and bulls (here made of gilt cast zinc), was held to be a Greek invention. Yet, as an element of antiquity's architectural legacy

39 The Staircase Hall (2.00.), 2009, looking east

GUIDED TOUR

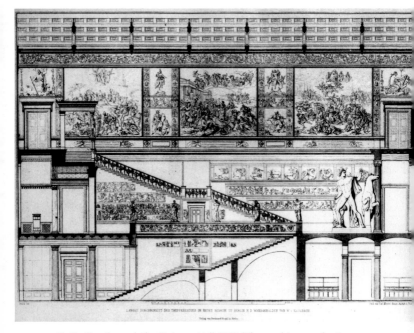

40 Section through the Staircase Hall, 1862, lithographic reproduction after Friedrich August Stüler

that contributed to the typology of the early Christian and Byzantine basilica, it ranked as an appropriate symbol of the transition from one world era to another, as represented by heathen Athens and Christian Ravenna (fig. 43). Such considerations doubtless mattered greatly to the deeply religious king of Prussia.

In 1992 the committee of experts from East and West Berlin unanimously stated that wartime bombing had rendered the Staircase Hall, with its subtle and complex artistic furnishings and decoration, an irretrievable loss. At the same time, the committee declared that reconstruction of the museum should not do away with the Hall's structural

41   Hedwig Schulz-Voelker, *The Grand Staircase Hall in the Neues Museum*,
c. 1910, watercolour, Staatliche Museen zu Berlin, Kupferstichkabinett

42 Karl Friedrich Schinkel, Proposal for a palace on the Acropolis in Athens, 1834, watercolour, Staatliche Museen zu Berlin, Kupferstichkabinett

function in the architectural organism of the museum as whole and should preserve Stüler's spatial articulation by means of 'long, simple flights of steps' running in opposing directions. This presented an almost insoluble problem: how to produce a spatial arrangement analogous to Stüler's stairs that incorporated surviving sections and reflected current ideas and constructional methods without lapsing into nostalgic imitation of individual features. Any recourse to details that had made sense in the context of the original whole would automatically entail the creation of a series of

43 Sant'Apollinare in Classe, Ravenna, sixth century

ultimately meaningless replicas. The first step towards rein-
terpreting the space involved substituting a few simple, bold
forms for the highly intricate aesthetic texture of the original, with its ornamental profusion. Thus, large sections of
polymer concrete, precisely abutted and matt-finished, have
replaced both the gilt balusters, with their filigree-like pal-
mettes and rosettes, and the block-like balustrades of white
marble. Fitted into the brick fabric, the concrete elements
form a kind of panelling on the side walls of the stairs and on
the landing wall, replacing the equally 'artificial' Pompeian

red of the original and evincing a strong tactile quality, notably in the round moulding of the handrails. The panels boldly echo the main lines of the flights of steps and provide an almost archaic-looking frame for the wooden, Erechtheion-style entrance to the Bacchus Room, which has survived (frontispiece and fig. 39). Chipperfield's rigorous new treatment of the staircase contrasts with the walls of the Hall, which lost their layer of decoration almost entirely and now appear as rhythmic arrangements of bare bricks. (Originally, there was a space for air to circulate between the brick fabric and the plaster-coated walls with the murals.) Casts of classical reliefs now once more enliven the lower area of the stairs,[13] generating, as in Stüler's day, the aura of an Antique collection of stone monuments.

A proposal to replace the destroyed wall paintings at the top of the Staircase Hall with Kaulbach's drawn cartoons for them, now in the Alte Nationalgalerie, Berlin, was rejected after intensive discussion. So was the suggestion that a contemporary artist be commissioned to paint new murals: decoration of a purely formal kind, it was felt, could not do justice to the space, while any form of programmatic statement was bound to be problematic in the present day and age. An attempt to accommodate desires for a historical approach by reconstructing the caryatid porch as an effective culminating point also ended in failure. Close investigation of the possibilities revealed that reproducing the Greek original as a model would be utterly inconsistent with the overall reinterpretation of the Staircase Hall and would also appear pointless when bereft of the original architectural, aesthetic and theoretical context.

Finally, the loss of the open wooden roof truss presented the architect with a particularly difficult challenge. It would not be possible to reproduce or to translate into modern materials either the intention of the original, with

44   The terrace of the Kiyomizu temple, Kyoto, seventeenth century

its foundations in neoclassical theories of architecture, or its
intricately decorative effect. On the other hand, the great
height and huge volume of the Staircase Hall could scarce-
ly be capped fittingly with a plain flat ceiling. Chipperfield
eventually opted for a heavy, open, tall structure of wood-
en quadrangular beams. This supports the saddle-back roof,
now single-layered and correspondingly thinner. Models for
this construction are to be found not in Greece, but in the
wooden architecture of Japan, in the twelfth-century Great
Buddha hall of the Tÿdai-Ji temple at Nara, for example,
which is possibly the largest wooden structure in all archi-

tecture, and in the seventeenth-century terrace of the Kiy-omizu temple in Kyoto (Fig. 44). Chipperfield, who has worked in Japan, and especially in Kyoto, since the late 1980s, has transferred the compelling force of such architecture to the Neues Museum. Although the truss may seem overpowering at first, it does grant the space the required gravity, in terms both of its massive heaviness and of a dignity not overburdened with pathos.

In its radical new guise the Staircase Hall will inevitably shock those who hanker after the splendour of the original architecture of 1862, with all its ideological and aesthetic trappings. Yet the visual and emotional power of Chipperfield's recreation is surely felt by all viewers, as it challenges them to engage with the building and its history.

MAIN FLOOR

The entire main floor was originally given over to a succession of splendid galleries intended 'for the display of as complete a collection as possible of plaster casts after classical antiquity and the best works of the Middle Ages and subsequent periods, so as to offer a historical survey of sculpture in its best products'.[14] Arriving in the Ionic columned hall from the ground floor, visitors turned right into the Greek Room (Griechischer Saal, 2.08.), which was reserved for the principal works of Greek art, including a polychrome reconstruction by Carl Boetticher of a temple pediment from Aegina and casts of the original Parthenon frieze, removed from Athens to the British Museum in London in the early nineteenth century by Lord Elgin. Richly ornamented bowstring girders spanned the full width of the room, which, like the Egyptian Court, was decorated with pictures of archaeological sites, this time with ten in Greece. Among the parts of the museum completely de-

45   The Greek Room (2.08.), 2009

stroyed, the Greek Room was redesigned by Chipperfield
without supports, a rigorous arrangement of concrete
beams replacing the bowstrings (fig. 45). Walking in a
clockwise direction, visitors originally continued into a
small connecting room with a cast of the famous *Laocoön*
group. Today, they move directly into the Apollo Room
(Apollosaal, 2.09.; fig. 46), named after the cast of the Apollo Belvedere once displayed here. Remodelled in bold, epic
forms, the room now houses the Amarna collection.
Through the doorway on the right visitors can pass via a
bridge to the platform in the new Egyptian Court, a 'sanc-

46 The Apollo Room (2.09.), 2009

tuary' containing portraits of the Akhenaton royal family
(fig. p. 96).

A narrow passage leads from the Apollo Room to the
octagonal, two-storey North Dome Room (Nordkuppelsaal),
conserved in a semi-ruinous state (2.10.; fig. 47). With its iron
lantern and sumptuously decorated walls, it still exudes the
aura of an ancient Roman sanctuary. The semicircular corner niches are capped by conches, while the side niches and
the corresponding areas containing the doorways to the
Apollo Room and the Room of the Niobids are rectangular
and arched. Statues stood in all the niches, in front of walls

47 The North Dome Room (2.10.), 2009, with the bust of Nefertiti

that have retained their original colour of green porphyry. The lunettes contain remains of paintings depicting the deeds of Greek heroes, each one an allegory of the triumph of civilisation over raw, demonic nature: Hercules triumphing over the Arcadian stag; Bellerophon, mounted on Pegasus, killing the Chimaera; Perseus freeing Andromeda; and Theseus slaying the Minotaur. Paintings of *genii* at play with animals holy to the gods, and with their attributes, can still be deciphered in the dome coffers. The world-famous bust of Nefertiti is displayed in the centre of the room, at the intersection of the sightlines.

The next room, the Room of the Niobids (Niobidensaal, 2.11.), is the best preserved of all. It takes its name from the casts of statues depicting Niobe and her fourteen dying children that once stood here (the original group is in the Uffizi, Florence). The portal in the room incorporates casts of two caryatids inspired by the corresponding figure in the Villa Albani, Rome, which Leo von Klenze had already used in his design for the entrance to the Roman gallery in the Glyptothek in Munich. The inscription above the portal, based on Aeschylus, invokes art as an essential component of human existence: 'Es schuf Prometheus jede Kunst den Sterblichen' (Prometheus created all art for mortals). The portal at the other end of the room, leading to the Bacchus Room, bears a German translation of the well-known sentence from Sophocles' tragedy *Antigone*: 'Many wonders there be, but none more wondrous than man.' Bowstring girders elaborately decorated with gilt zinc figures span the full width of the room and support the iron purlins on which the smooth, segmental vault rests (fig. 48). In accordance with Boetticher's structural theories, the points at which the bowstrings are anchored to the walls are masked by consoles that perform no load-bearing function. Formed like rope, the bowstrings illustrate in visual terms the thrusts and tensions at play in the construction. The paper covering the light-weight vault shows a stylised version of the terracotta pot ceiling behind it. Missing sections of the paper have been restored in a clearly visible way. Similarly, damaged areas in the Pompeian red of the walls have been brought into line with the original colour. The frieze around the top of the walls has survived in good condition. Some of its twenty-one paintings on sub-

48 The Room of the Niobids (2.11.), 2009, with entrance to the North Dome Room

jects from classical mythology were based on designs by the neoclassical painter Bonaventura Genelli (fig. 49).* Today, the Room of the Niobids houses a Library of Antiquity, displayed in four long table cases and comprising rolls of papyrus and

* The subjects are: Orpheus in the underworld; Cadmus slaying the dragon; Hypsipyle finding Opheltes/Archemoros killed by a snake; Mercury putting Argus to sleep; the banished Oedipus led out of Thebes by his daughter Antigone; Pelops and Hippodameia after winning the chariot race; Tantalus and Sisyphus in Hades; Jason and Medea with the Golden Fleece and the dead dragon; Diana saving Iphigenia from sacrifice; Achilles receiving new armour from Thetis over Patroclus' corpse; Odysseus saved by Leucothea's shawl; Aeneas fleeing from the burning Troy with Anchises and Ascanius; Daedalus making wings for Icarus;

49 Murals in the Room of the Niobids (2.11.), photographed in 1943

parchment, codices and illuminated manuscripts ranging from the classics of ancient Egypt to medieval Qurans.

The Bacchus Room (Bacchussaal, 2.01.), with its elaborate wooden portal leading to the Staircase Hall, marks the mid-point of the tour. Its lower section, beneath the upper landing of the Staircase Hall, is supported by an arcade, while the taller area, on the window side, has a flat ceiling. The original painted decoration depicted a vine arbour on a violet

Prometheus chained to the rock; Romulus ploughing; Ajax enraged; Meleager presenting Atalanta with the head of the Calydonian boar; Peleus abducting Thetis; Hyllus, son of Hercules, presenting his mother with the head of Eurystheus; Cecrops worshiping a statue of Athena; and Cheiron educating Achilles.

GUIDED TOUR

50 The Roman Room (2.02.), 2009

background. Remnants of this survive, as do some fine gro-
tesques on the pillars. Two Pompeian columns with painted mosaic ornaments mark the entrance to the Roman
Room (Römischer Saal, 2.02.). The original wall decoration
in this room, with its moss-green colour and its four poly-

chrome niches on the side abutting the Greek Court, is preserved in fragments. An elaborate portal of carved stucco stands at either end of the room. Arcades divide the space into four bays. Each arcade has two Ionic columns of Bohemian marble and appears between lateral barrel vaults constructed from terracotta pots (fig. 50). The light-blue, diamond-shaped stucco decoration of the vaults was modelled on ancient examples at Baalbek and in the palace of Diocletian at Split in Croatia. For the most part it has been conserved as preserved, only the geometrical lines being redrawn here and there. The mosaic floor has been repaired and restored. Paintings of Roman cities, landscapes and architectural sites by Eduard Pape form an impressive sequence around the upper zone of the walls and originally created a topographical and historical context for the works of art on display. The murals have been carefully conserved, but only sparingly restored, the missing areas merely rendered less conspicuous (figs. 51, 52).[*]

The South Dome Room (Südkuppelsaal, 2.03.) was destroyed entirely. This central-planned space with a top-lit dome on pendentives had been particularly striking, featuring large lunettes with paintings on subjects relating to the transition from classical antiquity to Christendom.[**] Visitors

[*] The surviving paintings show Trajan's forum, the Forum Romanum, the imperial palaces of Rome with the Circus Maximus, the arch of Constantine, the Porta Nigra in Trier, Pliny's stibadium at Tuscum and the gate of Pompei. The lost images depicted the columbarium of Livia Augusta, the tomb of the Plautian family at Tivoli, the Sibylla temple at Tivoli, the Isis temple in Pompei, the forum in Pompei, the island of Aesculap in the Tiber in Rome, the Villa Tiburtina of Trajan, the baths of Caracalla, the temple at Praeneste and the interior of the Scipio family tomb outside Rome.
[**] The paintings, executed to designs by Wilhelm von Kaulbach, depicted Emperor Constantine's conversion to Christianity, the consecration of Hagia Sofia in Constantinople by Emperor Justinian in 549, Theoderich receiving ambassadors from various nations in Ravenna and the reconciliation of Wit-

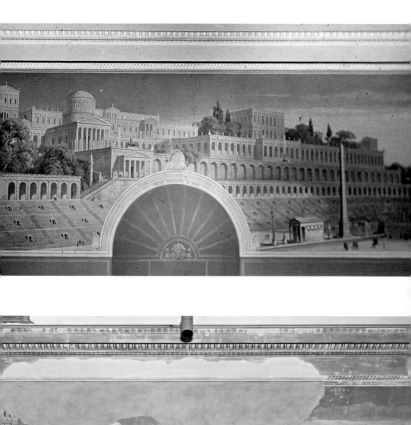

51, 52   Eduard Pape, *The Palatine with the Circus Maximus in Rome*, mural
in the Roman Room, photographed in 1943 (above) and 2008 (below)

53 The South Dome Room (2.03.), 2009

GUIDED TOUR

54 The Medieval Room (2.04.), 2009, with view of the South Dome Room

could pass through a screen of columns in the south and step onto the bridge leading to the Altes Museum. Chipperfield incorporated a lift for disabled access, emergency stairs and service areas in his new version of the south-east corner of the building, which is skewed very slightly to the south-west. His completely redesigned South Dome Room operates with exposed brick and shows an uninterrupted, but vibrant transition from the square floor plan to the oculus at the top. The space, lit by a glazed lantern, exudes an archaic aura (fig. 53).

tekind, duke of Saxony, with Charlemagne. On gold grounds, the tondi showed the four cardinal virtues with allegories of the four principal cities of the Middle Ages, Rome, Jerusalem, Byzantium/Constantinople and Aachen.

55 The Modern Room (collection of plaster casts), 1862, lithographic reproduction after Friedrich August Stüler

From the South Dome Room the tour moves to the former Medieval Room (Mittelalterlicher Saal, 2.04.; fig. 54). With nine flat domes supported by Ionic columns and pilasters, it repeats the basic structure of the Flat Dome Room beneath it. From the original series of portraits of medieval Holy Roman emperors only those of Maximilian I and Charles IV remain. The new exedra adopts the effective idea of a top-lit niche for what was originally a chapel-like sanctuary decorated with works of medieval Christian art (fig. 16).

The small room to the south-west of the Medieval Room, originally called the Bernward Room (Bernwardzimmer, 2.05.), housed works of art associated with the eponymous

56 The Modern Room (2.06.), 2009

57 The Modern Room (2.06.), 2005

art-loving bishop of Hildesheim. Today, it functions as a 'frag-
ment room' devised by Martin Reichert, Chipperfield's project architect. Large-scale architectural ornaments are
mounted on the walls like trophies, while a number of glass
cases from the Stüler building contain items recovered from
the ruins of the museum that could not be used in its reconstruction: remains of cast-iron and cast-zinc ornaments,
parts of floor mosaics, fragments of Kaulbach's murals, pots
from vaults, and other terracotta objects.

The original art historical survey ended in the Modern
Room (Moderner Saal, 2.06.). In a manner very similar to the
corresponding gallery in Munich's Glyptothek (the Saal der

Neueren), the display illustrated the continued presence or the revival of the legacy of classical antiquity and the Middle Ages through well-known works of art from the Renaissance to the nineteenth century – a time span then still seen as an entity. Six arcades with pairs of Ionic columns and a number of partition walls of the kind used by Schinkel in the picture gallery of the Altes Museum and by Klenze in his contemporaneous New Hermitage in St Petersburg divided the room into a series of 'booths'. These contained dense arrangements of statues and reliefs from various 'schools and epochs'. The Modern Room suffered severe damage but has now regained its basic historical shape (figs. 55, 56, 57). In addition, the plaster cast of Lorenzo Ghiberti's 'Gates of Paradise' from the Florence Baptistery has been reinstalled in its original position.

THE TOP FLOOR

The imposing flights of stairs in the Staircase Hall end on the top floor, which once housed the department of prints and drawings in the north and, until 1875, the *Kunstkammer* in the south. All load-bearing structures on this floor consisted of light-weight iron constructions. Reflecting its less heavy use, this storey originally had French parquet flooring. This has survived in the Star Room and the Majolika Room; elsewhere it has been replaced by oak boards. Decoration was markedly less lavish than on the other two storeys.

Today, the top floor is given over to the pre- and early history collection, which is displayed in a manner consonant with the relatively plain character of the galleries. From the upper landing, which offers an impressive view down into the Staircase Hall, visitors turn left into the Red Room (Roter Saal, 3.11.; fig. 58). With its restored Pompeian wall colour-

58 The Red Room (3.11.), 2009

ing and gold bowstring girders, this room represents a sim-
plified version of the Room of the Niobids beneath it. The
first bay, separated from the rest and containing stairs to the
garret spaces, once housed a room in which staff members
handed out prints and drawings for study purposes. Stüler's
bowstring girders can be seen here in their purely constructional 'core form'. The Red Room was formerly decorated with
portraits of famous printmakers and draughtsmen. Late-
nineteenth-century glass cases from the old Kunstgewerbemuseum have now been installed here to convey an impression of how objects used to be displayed in museums. Chris-

GUIDED TOUR

59 The Western Art Chamber (3.06.), 2009

tian Daniel Rauch's bust of Albrecht Dürer once again watches over the room from the niche in the end wall.

Skirting the empty space of the north-east dome, the visitor arrives in the former Green Room (Grüner Saal, 3.09.), which now belongs to the new north-west section of the building. A fine view of the Egyptian Court is to be had from here. The next room – originally the Blue Room (Blauer Saal, 3.08.) – is lit from both sides. One bay has been divided off from the rest, creating a small room corresponding to that once occupied by the director in this corner of the museum. The Blue Room housed Berlin's outstanding collection of

60 The Star Room (3.05.), 2009, with the 'Berlin Golden Hat'

some five thousand prints and drawings, made available to visitors here or in the Red Room on request.

Passing through an Ionic arcaded room, the visitor again has a spectacular view of the Staircase Hall before entering the Western Art Chamber (Westlicher Kunstkammersaal, 3.06.). This once contained 'curiosities and works produced by the art industry in the Middle Ages and more recent times, splendid ivories and woodcarvings, rare items of glass, porcelain etc.' Pillars of cast concrete, tapering slightly towards the bottom and supporting concrete beams, have replaced the destroyed cast-iron load-bearing system, which was deemed irreplacable (fig. 59). The whole brings to mind Josef Plečnik's unconventional classicism in the rooms he

61   The Majolika Room (3.04.), 2009

designed in the 1920s and 1930s for the President of Czechoslovakia in the Hradschin in Prague and for the library in Ljubljana.

The next room, the Star Room (Sternensaal, 3.05.; fig. 60), features an unusual Rabitz vault and was created as a period room suitable for the display of ecclesiatical treasures. Its reconstruction has already been described. The ceiling of the following space, the Majolika Room (Majolikasaal, 3.04.), echoes the flat domes of the two rooms beneath it (fig. 61). Preserved in their 'core forms', the light-weight iron structures and the terracotta pot domes now seem almost modern in their unvarnished appearance. Via a room in the new south-east corner, visitors reach the final room, the Eastern Art Chamber (Östlicher Kunstkammersaal, 3.02.). Affected by the severe damage done to the building's roof, this room is largely new, distinctively modern in its materials and formal vocabulary.

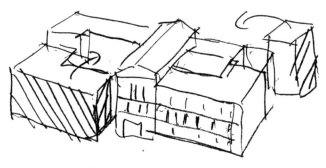

62 David Chipperfield, Sketch for the Neues Museum

ASSESSMENT

The debate over the rebuilding of the Neues Museum lasted more than two decades and was conducted with characteristic German thoroughness. It became the focus of an ideological dispute about the best way to approach our historical heritage. The nature of the various challenges posed by the derelict museum, and how best to meet them, were discussed with a vehemence probably unparalleled anywhere in recent years. In its new form the museum will continue to excite controversy because no visitor can escape the fascination of a building that exudes an aura both historical and contemporary. Architects, restorers and museum experts[15] have combined precise planning with both methodological reflection and artistic intuition to produce a New Museum that gives a new lease of life to Stüler's Neues Museum in two senses: it preserves as authentically as possible the historical fabric and the artistic ideas behind the original, and it grants them a new identity as part of a modern whole. This identity reflects current attitudes to the value, significance and presentation of the works of art on display and embodies changed intellectual horizons. In a completely novel way, the *mise en scène* of the treasures in the galleries casts new light on the relations between cultures and their development, of the forces of time and history and, not least, of the visual immediacy with which art overcomes those forces.

APPENDIX

THE ARCHITECTS

Friedrich August Stüler

Stüler was born in Mühlhausen in 1800, studied architecture at the Bauakademie in Berlin from 1818 to 1827 and subsequently worked for a while with Karl Friedrich Schinkel, whose goals he was to make his own. In 1824 he co-founded the Berlin Architektenverein, the local architects' association, and from 1829 to 1831 travelled in France, Italy and Russia. He was appointed Prussian court architect in 1832 and architect to the king in 1842. Along with the overall development plan for the 'Freistätte for Art and Science' in Berlin, comprising the Neues Museum and the National-galerie (for which he drew up preliminary designs), his most important works included the church of St Peter and St Paul in Nikolskoe, Komandors-ki Islands (1833–36), the dome and chapel of the Stadtschloss in Berlin (1845–53), the university of Königsberg (now Kaliningrad, 1843–62), the Bethanien hospital (now the Künstlerhaus) in Kreuzberg, Berlin (1845–47), the Matthäi-Kirche, Tiergarten, Berlin (1844–66), the National Museum in Stockholm (1847–66), the Orangery palace in Potsdam (1850–60), the Garde du Corps barracks opposite Charlottenburg palace in Berlin (1851–59, now home to the Museum Berggruen and the Scharf-Gerstenberg Collection), the former Wallraff-Richartz Museum in Cologne (1855–61) and the Academy of Sciences in Budapest (1862–65). He also completed buildings designed by Schinkel and Friedrich Ludwig Persius, including the Nikolaikirche and the Friedenskirche in Potsdam. In addition, he rebuilt, remodelled, decorated or restored more than three hundred churches, dozens of palaces, mansions, residential and commercial buildings, monuments, tombs, barracks and railway stations in Berlin, Brandenburg and all Prussian possessions, including the Rhineland and Silesia (now Poland). Stüler, who died in Berlin in 1865, was one of the most important German architects in the transition from neoclassicism to historicism.

David Chipperfield

David Chipperfield was born in London in 1953. After studying at Kingston School of Art and the Architectural Association in London he worked in the practices of Douglas Stephen, Richard Rogers and Norman Foster. In 1984 he set up David Chipperfield Architects, which today maintains a staff of about 150 in London, Berlin, Milan and Shanghai. The practice has won more than forty national and international competitions and received many international awards, among them the RIBA Stirling Prize in 2007. Chipperfield teaches in Europe and the USA. In addition to the Neues Museum in Berlin, major works by him in Germany include the Deutsches Literaturarchiv's Museum of Modern Literature in Marbach (2006), the Am Kupfergraben 10 art gallery in Berlin (2006–07) and the extension to the Museum Folkwang in Essen (begun in 2007).

Julian Harrap

Julian Harrap was born in Essex in 1942. He studied architecture in London under Sir Lesley Martin, Sir James Sterling and Colin St John Wilson. He set up on his own after six years of working in architecture practices. Harrap places his profound knowledge and understanding of planning, technology and materials at the service of preserving historic buildings. He is a member of various conservation bodies and cultural organisations in Britain and lectures regularly throughout Europe on the theory and practice of conservation and restoration. For the past ten years Harrap has acted as design consultant on historic buildings for the Royal Academy of Arts. Major commissions have involved Sir John Soane's Museum and Pitzhanger Manor in London and buildings by Nicholas Hawksmoor, Sir John Vanbrugh, Sir Charles Barry and John Nash.

BIBLIOGRAPHY

Friedrich August Stüler, *Bauwerke von A. Stüler*, part 1: *Das Neue Museum in Berlin (24 Tafeln)*, Berlin, 1862.

Richard Lepsius, *Königliche Museen: Abtheilung der Ägyptischen Alterthümer – Die Wandgemälde der verschiedenen Räume*, Berlin, 1855.

Günther Schade, *Die Berliner Museumsinsel: Zerstörung, Rettung, Wiederaufbau*, Berlin, 1986.

Werner Busch, 'Wilhelm von Kaulbach, peintre-philosophe und modern painter: Zu Kaulbachs Weltgeschichtszyklus im Berliner Neuen Museum', in *Welt und Wirkung von Hegels Ästhetik*, Hegel-Studien, suppl. 27, Bonn, 1986, pp. 117–38.

Hartmut Dorgerloh, 'Die museale Inszenierung der Kunstgeschichte: Das Bild- und Ausstattungsprogramm des Neuen Museums zu Berlin', diploma thesis, Humboldt-Universität, Berlin, 1987.

M. Mutscher, 'Das Neue Museum von F. A. Stüler als ein Höhepunkt der klassizistischen Architekturentwicklung: Ein Beispiel für neue Baugestaltungs- und Konstruktionsziele des 19. Jahrhunderts', 2 vols., Ph.D. thesis, Technische Universität, Dresden, 1988.

Hartmut Dorgerloh, '"Eine Schöpfung von grossem Reichthum poetischer Erfindung": Der Relieffries "Die Zerstörung Pompejis" von Hermann Schievelbein im Griechischen Hof des Neuen Museums', *Staatliche Museen zu Berlin: Forschungen und Berichte*, vol. 31, 1991, pp. 281–92.

Annemarie Menke-Schwinghammer, *Weltgeschichte als Nationalepos: Wilhelm von Kaulbachs kulturhistorischer Zyklus im Treppenhaus des Neuen Museums in Berlin*, Berlin, 1994.

Senatsverwaltung für Stadtentwicklung und Umweltschutz, *Das Neue Museum in Berlin: Ein denkmalpflegerisches Plädoyer zur ergänzenden Wiederherstellung*, Beiträge zur Denkmalpflege in Berlin, vol. 1, Berlin, 1994.

Bundesbaudirektion, *Museumsinsel Berlin: Wettbewerb zum Neuen Museum*, Stuttgart, Berlin and Paris, 1994.

Thomas Gaehtgens, *Die Berliner Museumsinsel im deutschen Kaiserreich*, Munich, 1992.

Hartmut Dorgerloh, Monika Wagner, Werner Lorenz, Anke Borgmeyer, Jörg Haspel et al., 'Stülers Neues Museum und die Spreeinsel als

Forum für die preußische Residenzstadt', in Zentralinstitut für Kunstgeschichte, Munich, ed., *Berlins Museen: Geschichte und Zukunft*, Munich and Berlin, 1994, pp. 79–154.

Werner Lorenz, 'Stülers Neues Museum: Ikunabel preußischer Konstruktionskunst im Zeichen der Industrialisierung', in Zentralinstitut für Kunstgeschichte, Munich, ed., *Berlins Museen: Geschichte und Zukunft*, Munich and Berlin, 1994, pp. 99–112.

Eva Börsch-Supan, 'Das Neue Museum in Berlin: Über den Umgang mit einem Baudenkmal', *Die Denkmalpflege*, vol. 53, no. 1, 1995, pp. 5–21.

Adrian von Buttlar, 'Erhaltungsziel Museumsinsel'; Dietrich Wildung, 'Der Denkmalbegriff eines Denkmalpflegers'; and Achim Hubel, 'Der Denkmalbegriff eines Archäologen?', *Kunstchronik*, no. 8, 1997, pp. 391–96; no. 12, 1997, pp. 679–81; and no. 1, 1998, pp. 45–46.

Eva Börsch-Supan and Dietrich Müller-Stüler, *Friedrich August Stüler 1800–1865*, Munich and Berlin, 1997.

Staatliche Museen zu Berlin – Stiftung Preußischer Kulturbesitz (Andres Lepik), *Masterplan Museumsinsel Berlin: Ein europäisches Projekt*, Berlin, 2000.

Elsa van Wezel, 'Die Konzeptionen des Alten und Neuen Museums zu Berlin und das sich wandelnde historische Bewusstsein', *Jahrbuch der Berliner Museen*, vol. 43, 2001, suppl., part 2, pp. 111–222.

Falk Jäger, 'Intervention auf leisen Sohlen: Der Londoner Architekt David Chipperfield' and 'Gedanken von David Chipperfield zum Masterplan', in Carola Wedel, ed., *Die neue Museumsinsel: Der Mythos, der Plan, die Vision*, Berlin, 2002, pp. 144–48 and 148–56.

David Chipperfield, 'Das Neue Museum', *Jahrbuch Preußischer Kulturbesitz*, vol. 40, 2003, pp. 83–107.

David Chipperfield, *Neues Museum: Dokumentation und Planung*, Berlin, 2003.

Das Neue Museum in Berlin: Konzeption der Gesellschaft Historisches Berlin zum Wiederaufbau der Treppenhalle, text by Christa Sammler, Berlin, 2005.

Eva Heinecke, 'Studien zum Neuen Museum in Berlin 1841–1860: Baugeschichte, Verantwortliche, Nordische und Ägyptische Abteilung, Geschichtskonzept', unpubl. Ph.D. thesis, Technische Universität, Berlin, 2006.

Bénédicte Savoy, ed., *Tempel der Kunst: Die Geburt des öffentlichen Museums in Deutschland 1701–1815*, Mainz, 2006.

Das Neue Museum, Berlin: Der Bauzustand um 1990, photographs by
Andres Kilger, text by Bernhard Maaz, Berlin, 2009.

Das Neue Museum (Berlin), in Wikipedia
http://de.wikipedia.org/wiki/Neues_Museum_(Berlin)

Kaye Geipel, Jürgen Tietz, Nikolaus Bernau and Georg Mörsch, 'Das Neue
Museum in Berlin', *Bauwelt*, vol. 13, 2009, pp. 14–37.

Staatliche Museen zu Berlin – Stiftung Preußischer Kulturbesitz,
*The Neues Museum Berlin: conserving, restoring, rebuilding within the
World Heritage*, ed. Oliver G. Hamm, Leipzig, 2009.

Staatliche Museen zu Berlin – Stiftung Preußischer Kulturbesitz/
Elke Blauert, *Neues Museum: Architektur, Sammlung, Geschichte*,
Berlin, 2009.

NOTES

[1] See Leo von Klenze, *Aphoristische Bemerkungen, gesammelt auf seiner Reise
in Griechenland, mit einem Tafelatlas*, Berlin, 1838, and a painting by the architect in the State Hermitage Museum, St Petersburg (1835; fig. 6); also
Adrian von Buttlar, *Leo von Klenze: Leben ,Werk, Vision*, Munich, 1999.

[2] In 1868 Boetticher (1806–1889) became director of the Berlin sculpture
collection, which included the plaster casts displayed in the Neues Museum.

[3] The stages in between were Homer and the flowering of Greece, the destruction of Jerusalem, the battle of the Catalaunian plains and the cru-
saders before Jerusalem. Further paintings, with gold grounds, showed allegories of mythology, history, art and science, images of Solon the great
law-maker (in conjunction with Venus), Moses (with Isis), Charlemagne (with
a personification of Italy) and Frederick II of Hohenstaufen (with a personification of Germany).

[4] The other members of the committee were Ernst Badstübner, Hartmut
Dorgerloh, August Gebessler, Thomas Mader, Helmut F. Reichwald and Man-
fred Schuller.

[5] Represented by Jörg Haspel, *Landeskonservator*; Frank Pieter Hesse, *Konservator*; and Norbert Heuler, *Konservator*.

[6] Represented by Florian Mausbach, president; Barbara Grosse-Rhode, *Ref-
erentin*; and Eva Maria Niemann, project manager.

[7] Alexander Schwarz, Design Director; Martin Reichert and Eva Schad, Project Architects; and, in the field of conservation and restoration, Wulfgang Henze (Bundesamt für Bauwesen und Raumordnung), Project Manager, and many well-known specialist restorers and firms.

[8] See Staatliche Museen zu Berlin – Stiftung Preußischer Kulturbesitz, *Das Neue Museum Berlin*, 2009.

[9] Elsa van Wezel, 2001.

[10] The six missing paintings depicted the Hathor temple and the 'typhonium' at Dendera, the Ramesseum and Memnon statues in Thebes, the temple of Gerf Hussein, the rock-cut tombs at Beni Hasan, the pyramids of Gizeh and a view of Meroe.

[11] Pluto, lord of the underworld, sits on a monster representing Vesuvius, while Helios (the sun) and Luna (the moon) descend in their chariots, retreating from the darkness. The image was based on the popular novel *The Last Days of Pompeii* by Edward Bulwer Lytton (1803–1873), published in London in 1836 and issued in German translation in Potsdam in 1837 with a commentary by Friedrich Förster, a member of staff of the royal *Kunstkammer*. For contemporaries, the destruction of Pompeii and Herculaneum marked the transition from the heathen world of antiquity to the early Christian period.

[12] The sources used were Jacob Grimm, *Deutsche Mythologie*, Berlin, 1834 (2nd ed., 1844), and August Schrader, *Germanische Mythologie*, Berlin, 1843. The murals were painted by Robert Müller, Gustav Heidenreich and Gustav Richter, their designs amended by Wilhelm von Kaulbach.

[13] Metopes and frieze fragments from the Parthenon and the Hephaisteion in Athens and from the mausoleum of Halicarnassus and the Nereid monument in Xanthos.

[14] Stüler, 1862.

[15] Dietrich Wildung (Ägyptisches Museum and Papyrus collection), Andreas Scholl and Martin Maischberger (Antikensammlung), Wilfried Menghin and Matthias Wemhoff (Museum für Vor- und Frühgeschichte).

PHOTOGRAPHIC ACKNOWLEDGEMENTS

p. 2   Staircase Hall (2.00.), 2009

p. 4   View of the North Dome
Room (2.10.) from the Room
of the Niobids (2.11.), 2009

p. 96   The platform in the Egyptian Court (2.12.)

© Jürgen Albrecht
figs. 25, 53

© bpk / Reinhard Görner
p. 2 and figs. 48, 50, 61

© bpk / Achim Kleuker
figs. 38, 45, 58

© bpk / Andrea Kroth
fig. 46

© bpk / Kunstbibliothek, SMB /
Dietmar Katz
fig. 56

© bpk / Kupferstichkabinett, SMB
fig. 3

© bpk / Kupferstichkabinett, SMB /
Jörg P. Anders
figs. 2, 11, 41, 42

© bpk / Linus Lintner
p. 96 and figs. 29, 47, 60

© bpk / Hermann Rückwardt
fig. 4

© bpk / Scala
fig. 43

© bpk / Stiftung Preußischer
Kulturbesitz, ART+COM
fig. 15

© bpk / Zentralarchiv, SMB
figs. 7, 9, 13, 40

© bpk / Zentralarchiv, SMB /
Knud Petersen
fig. 14

© Jörg von Bruchhausen
figs. 10, 23, 24, 30, 34, 54

© Adrian von Buttlar
fig. 44

© David Chipperfield Architects
figs. 5, 21, 27, 36, 62

© Otto Cürlis / Zentralinstitut für
Kunstgeschichte – Photothek
für die Bundesrepublik
Deutschland
figs. 49, 51

© Markus Hilbich
fig. 20

© Johannes Kramer
figs. 18, 31, 32, 52, 56, 57

© BLDAM, Bildarchiv,
Neg.-Nr. 20c8/1473.6
back cover

© Christian Richters
figs. 1, 16, 22, 26, 31, 39, 59

© Peter Thieme / BBR
fig. 35

© Stiftung Preußischer Kulturbesitz / ART+COM
fig. 19

© Stiftung Preußischer Kulturbesitz / David Chipperfield
Architects, photographer: Ute
Zscharnt
front cover, p. 4 and figs. 12, 37

© Stiftung Preußischer Kulturbesitz / Imaging Atelier
fig. 17

© The State Hermitage Museum
fig. 6

© Tomasz Tarczynski
fig. 33

The publishers wish to thank the author, the photographers, all those
who have provided photographs and the staff of David Chipperfield
Architects, especially Martin Reichert, Maria Zedler and Nina Helten, for
their generous cooperation.

Bibliografische Information der Deutschen Nationalbibliothek

Die Deutsche Nationalbibliothek verzeichnet diese Publikation in der
Deutschen Nationalbibliografie; detaillierte bibliografische Daten sind im
Internet über http://dnb.d-nb.de abrufbar.

German text copy-edited by Martin Steinbrück
Translated by Michael Foster, Munich
Proofread by Catherine Framm, Berlin
Production coordinated by Jens Möbius
Designed by Barbara Criée, Berlin
Reproductions by bildpunkt, Berlin
Printed and bound by MEDIALIS Offsetdruck, Berlin

© 2010 Staatliche Museen zu Berlin and Deutscher Kunstverlag GmbH
Berlin München
ISBN 978-3-422-06980-0